Your

HAPPILY EVER AFTER

Your
HAPPILY EVER AFTER

DIETER F. UCHTDORF

DESERET
BOOK

SALT LAKE CITY, UTAH

Adapted from Dieter F. Uchtdorf, "Your Happily Ever After," *Ensign,* May 2010, 124–27.

Photograph of Dieter and Harriet Uchtdorf on page 29 was taken by Doug Holladay and is used courtesy of the author.
Interior illustrations © Dementeva Marina & Natasha NaSt/Shutterstock
Interior design by Sheryl Dickert Smith

(CIP on file)
ISBN 978-1-60641-652-5

Printed in the United States of America
Worzalla Publishing Co., Stevens Point, WI
10   9   8   7   6   5   4   3   2   1

CONTENTS

*O*ver the years I have been exposed to many beautiful languages—each of them is fascinating and remarkable; each has its particular charm. But as different as these languages can be, they often have things in common. For example, in most languages there exists a phrase as magical and full of promise as perhaps any in the world.

THAT PHRASE IS

Once upon a time.

Aren't those wonderful words to begin a story? *"Once upon a time"* promises something: a story of adventure and romance, a story of princesses and princes. It may include tales of courage, hope, and everlasting love. In many of these stories, nice overcomes mean and good overcomes evil. But perhaps most of all, I love it when we turn to the last page and our eyes reach the final lines and we see the enchanting words *"And they lived happily ever after."*

Isn't that what we all desire: to be the heroes and heroines of our own stories; to triumph over adversity; to experience life in all its beauty; and, in the end, to live happily ever after?

Today I want to draw your attention to something very significant, very extraordinary. On the first page of the *Young Women Personal Progress* book, you will find these words:

"You are a beloved daughter of Heavenly Father, prepared to come to the earth at this particular time for a sacred and glorious purpose."[1]

Sisters, those words are true! They are not made up in a fairy tale! Isn't it remarkable to know that our eternal Heavenly Father knows you, hears you, watches over you, and loves you with an infinite love? In fact, His love for you is so great that He has granted you this earthly life as a precious gift of "once upon a time," complete with your own true story of adventure, trial, and opportunities for greatness, nobility, courage, and love. And, most glorious of all, He offers you a gift beyond price and comprehension. Heavenly Father offers to you the greatest gift of all—eternal life—and the opportunity and infinite blessing of your own "happily ever after."

But such a blessing does not come without a price. It is not given simply because you desire it. It comes only through understanding who you are and what you must become in order to be worthy of such a gift.

chapter one

TRIAL IS
PART OF THE
JOURNEY

For a moment, think back about your favorite fairy tale. In that story the main character may be a princess or a peasant; she might be a mermaid or a milkmaid, a ruler or a servant. You will find one thing all have in common: they must overcome adversity.

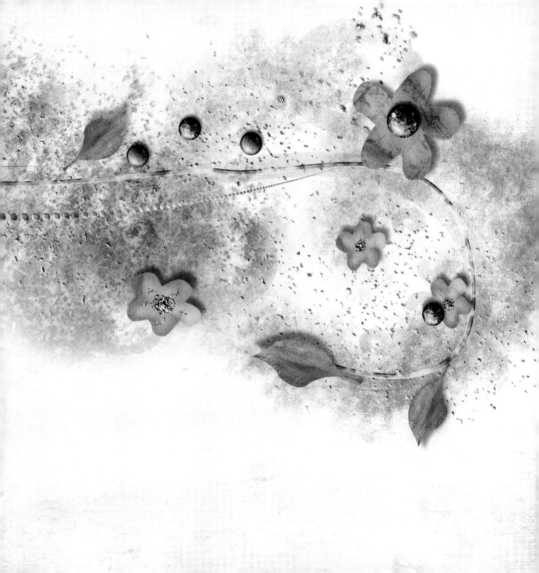

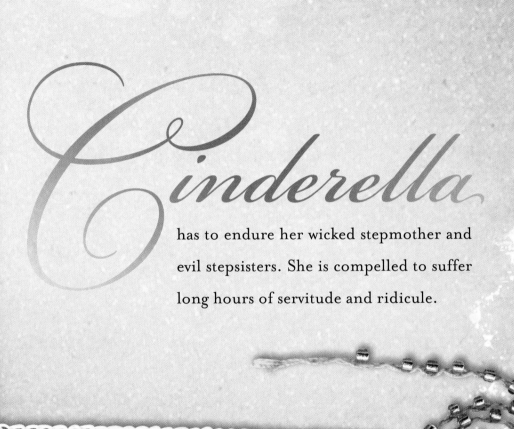

Cinderella

has to endure her wicked stepmother and evil stepsisters. She is compelled to suffer long hours of servitude and ridicule.

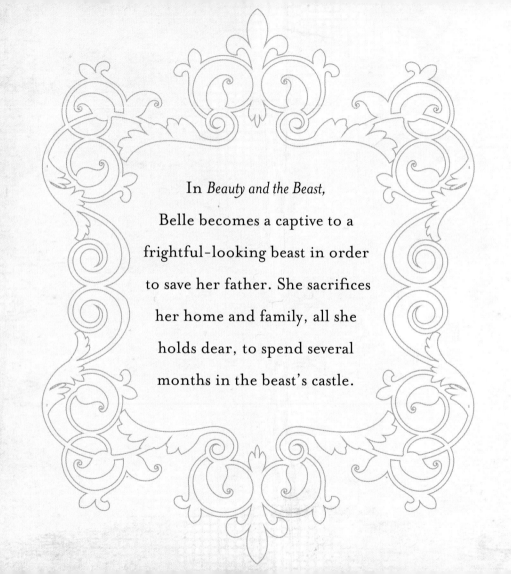

In *Beauty and the Beast,*
Belle becomes a captive to a
frightful-looking beast in order
to save her father. She sacrifices
her home and family, all she
holds dear, to spend several
months in the beast's castle.

In the tale "Rumpelstiltskin," a poor miller promises the king that his daughter can spin straw into gold. The king immediately sends for her and locks her in a room with a mound of straw and a spinning wheel. Later in the story she faces the danger of losing her firstborn child unless she can guess the name of the magical creature who helped her in this impossible task.

In each of these stories, Cinderella, Belle, and the miller's daughter have to experience sadness and trial before they can reach their "happily ever after."

Think about it.

HAS THERE EVER BEEN A PERSON WHO DID NOT HAVE TO GO THROUGH HIS OR HER OWN DARK VALLEY OF TEMPTATION, TRIAL, AND SORROW?

Sandwiched between their *once upon a time* and

happily ever after, they all had to experience great

adversity. Why must all experience sadness and tragedy?

Why could we not simply live in bliss and peace, each day

filled with wonder, joy, and love?

The scriptures tell us there must be opposition in all things, for without it we could not discern the sweet from the bitter.[2] Would the marathon runner feel the triumph of finishing the race had she not felt the pain of the hours of pushing against her limits? Would the pianist feel the joy of mastering an intricate sonata without the painstaking hours of practice?

In stories, as in life, adversity teaches us things we cannot learn otherwise.

Adversity helps to develop a depth of character that comes in no other way. Our loving Heavenly Father has set us in a world filled with challenges and trials so that we, through opposition, can learn wisdom, become stronger, and experience joy.

One Sunday the missionaries brought a new family to our meetings whom I hadn't seen before. It was a mother with two beautiful daughters. I thought that these missionaries were doing a very, very good job.

I particularly took notice of the one daughter with gorgeous dark hair and large brown eyes. Her name was Harriet, and I think I fell in love with her from the first moment I saw her. Unfortunately, this beautiful young woman didn't seem to feel the same about me. She had many young men who wanted to make her acquaintance, and I began to wonder if she would ever see me as anything but a friend. But I didn't let that deter me. I figured out ways to be where she was. When I passed the sacrament, I made sure I was in the right position so that I would be the one to pass the sacrament to her.

When we had special activities at church, I rode my bike to Harriet's house and rang the doorbell. Harriet's mother usually answered. In fact, she opened the kitchen window of their apartment on the fourth floor and asked what I wanted. I would ask if Harriet would like a ride to church on my bicycle. Harriet's mother would say, "No, she will be coming later, but I will be happy to ride with you to church." This wasn't exactly what I had in mind, but how could I decline?

And so we rode to church. I must admit I had a very impressive road bike. Harriet's mother sat on the top tube bar just in front of me, and I tried to be the most elegant bicycle driver over roads of rough cobblestone.

Time passed. While beautiful Harriet was seeing many other young men, it seemed that I could not make any headway with her.

Was I disappointed? **Yes.**

Was I defeated?

Absolutely not!

Actually, looking back I recognize that it doesn't hurt at all to be on good terms with the mother of the girl of your dreams.

Years later, after I had finished my training as a fighter pilot in the air force, I experienced a modern miracle in Harriet's response to my continued court- ing. One day she said, "Dieter, you have matured much over these past years."

I moved quickly after that, and within a few months I was married to the woman I had loved ever since I first saw her. The process hadn't been easy—there were moments of suffering and despair—but finally my happiness was full, and it still is, even more so.

My dear young sisters, you need to know that you will experience your own adversity. None is exempt. You will suffer, be tempted, and make mistakes.

You will learn for yourself what every heroine has learned: through overcoming challenges come growth and strength.

It is your reaction to adversity,

not the adversity itself,

that determines how your

Life's story will develop.

There are those among you who, although young, have already suffered a full measure of grief and sorrow. My heart is filled with compassion and love for you. How dear you are to the Church. How beloved you are of your Heavenly Father. Though it may seem that you are alone, angels attend you. Though you may feel that no one can understand the depth of your despair, our Savior, Jesus Christ, understands. He suffered more than we can possibly imagine, and He did it for us; He did it for you. You are not alone.

If you ever feel your burden is too great to bear, lift your heart to your Heavenly Father, and He will uphold and bless you. He says to you, as He said to Joseph Smith, "[Your] adversity and [your] afflictions shall be but a small moment; and then, if [you] endure it well, God shall exalt [you] on high."[3]

Enduring adversity is not the only thing you must do to experience a happy life. Let me repeat: how you react to adversity and temptation is a critical factor in whether or not you arrive at your own *"happily ever after."*

chapter two

STAY TRUE TO WHAT YOU KNOW IS RIGHT

SISTERS, YOUNG SISTERS,

BELOVED YOUNG SISTERS,

*stay true to what you
know is right.*

*E*verywhere you look today, you will find promises of happiness. Ads in magazines promise total bliss if you will only buy a certain outfit, shampoo, or makeup. Certain media productions glamorize those who embrace evil or who give in to base instincts. Often these same people are portrayed as models of success and accomplishment.

In a world where evil is portrayed as good and good as evil, sometimes it is difficult to know the truth. In some ways it is almost like Little Red Riding Hood's dilemma: when you are not quite sure what you are seeing, is it a beloved grandmother or is it a dangerous wolf?

I spent many years in the cockpit of an airplane. My task was to get a big jet safely from any part of the world to our desired destination. I knew with certainty that if I wanted to travel from New York to Rome, I needed to fly east. If some were to tell me that I should fly south, I knew there was no truth in their words. I would not trust them because I knew for myself. No amount of persuasion, no amount of flattery, bribery, or threats could convince me that flying south would get me to my destination because I knew.

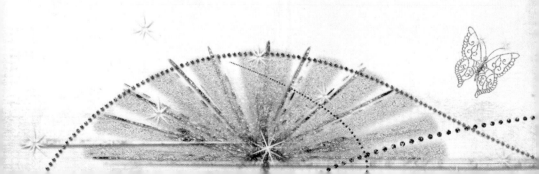

We all search for happiness, and we all try to find our own "happily ever after." The truth is, *God knows how to get there!* And He has created a map for you; He knows the way. He is your beloved Heavenly Father, who seeks your good, your happiness. He desires with all the love of a perfect and pure Father that you reach your supernal destination. *The map is available to all.* It gives explicit directions of what to do and where to go to everyone who is striving to come unto Christ and "stand as [a witness] of God at all times and in all things, and in all places."[4]

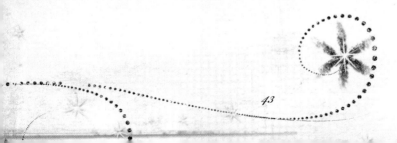

All you have to

do is trust your

Heavenly

Father.

TRUST HIM ENOUGH
TO FOLLOW HIS PLAN.

Nevertheless, not all will follow the map. They may look at it. They may think it is reasonable, perhaps even true. But they do not follow the divine directions. Many believe that any road will take them to a "happily ever after." Some may even become angry when others who know the way try to help and tell them. They suppose that such advice is outdated, irrelevant, out of touch with modern life.

Sisters, they suppose wrong.

chapter three

THE GOSPEL IS
THE WAY TO
HAPPILY EVER AFTER

I understand that, at times, some may wonder why they attend Church meetings or why it is so important to read the scriptures regularly or pray to our Heavenly Father daily. Here is my answer: You do these things because they are part of God's path for you.

And that path will take you
to your *"happily ever after"*
destination.

"Happily ever after" is not something found only in fairy tales. You can have it! It is available for you! But you must follow your Heavenly Father's map.

Sisters, please embrace the gospel of Jesus Christ! Learn to love your Heavenly Father with all your heart, might, and mind. Fill your souls with virtue, and love goodness. Always strive to bring out the best in yourself and others.

Learn to accept and act upon the Young Women values. Live the standards in *For the Strength of Youth*. These standards guide and direct you to your "happily ever after." Living these standards will prepare you to make sacred covenants in the temple and establish your own legacy of goodness in your individual circumstances. "Stand . . . in holy places, and be not moved,"[5] regardless of temptations or difficulties. I promise you that future generations will be grateful for you and praise your name for your courage and faithfulness during this crucial time of your life.

My dear sisters—you who stand for truth and righteousness, you who seek goodness, you who have entered the waters of baptism and walk in the ways of the Lord—our Father in Heaven has promised that you will "mount up with wings as eagles; [you] shall run, and not be weary; and [you] shall walk, and not faint."[6] You "shall not be deceived."[7] God will bless and prosper you.[8] "The gates of hell shall not prevail against you; . . . and the Lord God will disperse the powers of darkness from before you, and cause the heavens to shake for your good, and his name's glory."[9]

Sisters, we love you. We pray for you. Be strong and of good courage. You are truly royal spirit daughters of Almighty God. You are princesses, destined to become queens. Your own wondrous story has already begun.

YOUR

Once upon a time IS NOW.

As an Apostle of the Lord Jesus Christ, I leave you my blessing and give you a promise that as you accept and live the values and principles of the restored gospel of Jesus Christ, "[you] will be prepared to strengthen home and family, make and keep sacred covenants, receive the ordinances of the temple, and enjoy the blessings of exaltation."[10] And the day will come when you turn the final pages of your own glorious story; there you will read and experience the fulfillment of those blessed and wonderful words:

AND THEY LIVED

Happily Ever After.

1. *Young Women Personal Progress* (Salt Lake City: The Church of Jesus Christ of Latter-day Saints, 2009), 1.

2. 2 Nephi 2:11, 15.

3. Doctrine and Covenants 121:7–8.

4. Mosiah 18:9.

5. Doctrine and Covenants 87:8.

6. Isaiah 40:31.

7. Joseph Smith—Matthew 1:37.

8. See Mosiah 2:22–24.

9. Doctrine and Covenants 21:6.

10. *Young Women Personal Progress,* 3.

About the Author

President Dieter F. Uchtdorf has served as the Second Counselor in the First Presidency of The Church of Jesus Christ of Latter-day Saints since February 3, 2008. He was sustained as a member of the Quorum of the Twelve Apostles in October 2004. He became a General Authority in April 1994 and served as a member of the Presidency of the Seventy from August 2002 until his call to the Twelve.

Prior to his calling as a General Authority, President Uchtdorf was the senior vice president of flight operations and chief pilot of Lufthansa German Airlines.

President Uchtdorf was born in 1940 in what is now the Czech Republic. He grew up in Zwickau, Germany, where his family joined the Church in 1947. He and his wife, Harriet Reich Uchtdorf, are the parents of two children and have six grandchildren.